S is for STITCH

*52 Embroidered Alphabet Designs
+ Charming Projects for Little Ones*

KRISTYNE CZEPURYK

stashBOOKS®

an imprint of C&T Publishing

Text copyright © 2012 by Kristyne Czepuryk

Photography and Artwork copyright © 2012 by C&T Publishing, Inc.

Publisher: Amy Marson

Creative Director: Gailen Runge

Art Director/Book Designer: Kristy Zacharias

Editor: Liz Aneloski

Technical Editors: Helen Frost and Amanda Siegfried

Page Layout Artist: Kerry Graham

Production Coordinator: Zinnia Heinzmann

Production Editors: S. Michele Fry and Joanna Burgarino

Illustrators: Mary Flynn and Jessica Jenkins

Photography by Diane Pedersen and Cara Pardo of C&T Publishing, Inc., unless otherwise noted

Published by Stash Books, an imprint of C&T Publishing, Inc., P.O. Box 1456, Lafayette, CA 94549

Library of Congress Cataloging-in-Publication Data

Czepuryk, Kristyne, 1967-

S is for stitch : 52 embroidered alphabet designs + charming projects for little ones / Kristyne Czepuryk.

pages cm

ISBN 978-1-60705-651-5 (soft cover)

1. Embroidery--Patterns. 2. Patchwork--Patterns. 3. Quilting--Patterns. 4. Embroidery for children. 5. Alphabets. I. Title.

TT771.C96 2012

746.44--dc23

2012019274

Printed in China

10 9 8 7 6 5 4 3 2 1

DEDICATION

To my beautiful girls, Anna Mae and Holly— the inspirations behind this book and the most precious little people I've ever known.

To John—for ... everything.

To Mom—watching you take the time to do things right finally rubbed off on me.

To Kate—hand-holder and butt-kicker.

And to Dad—who always told me I could write my own patterns.

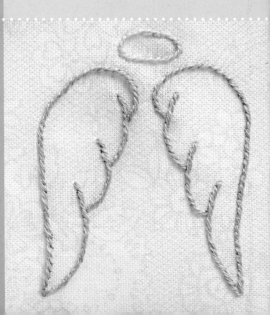

ACKNOWLEDGMENTS

Rome was not built in a day, and neither was this book. A lot of people helped my ideas get into your hands.

Nireko and Lecien—this book and my designs are beautiful because of your incredible fabrics and exceptional embroidery floss.

Special thanks to Annie at Pinks & Needles for the exquisite decorative pins (page 34).

Birgitte—thank you for giving me Tara Frey's book. It changed the direction of my life.

Susanne—I will always remember your kindness and enthusiasm for my work.

Angela—thank you for answering my 911 call. Your longarm quilting talents are a-ma-zing!

C&T Team—Amy, Gailen, Liz, Helen, Amanda, Kerry, Kristy, Zinnia, Michele, Mary, Diane, Cara … you guys rock.

CONTENTS

PREFACE

My big sister was given a needlepoint canvas kit of a purple elephant standing on grass in the sun. I begged her to let me do some stitches. (We had a very typical big sister–little sister relationship.) She finally gave in to my pleading and let me to do one yellow stitch in the sun, in the corner—that was my first stitch.

Later, when I was in Brownies, I made a pink felt mushroom pincushion decorated with French knots. I also remember a Holly Hobbie tapestry kit that I got for Christmas.

My mom bought me a kit to make a pillow with candlewicking—a form of white-work embroidery that traditionally uses unbleached cotton thread on a piece of unbleached muslin. It was decidedly nonbeginner, with padded satin stitches and bullion knots. My mom entered that pillow into a fall fair and it won second place. I was about twelve years old, and I seemed to have a knack for embroidery.

My first home economics assignment in eighth grade was a simple patchwork pillow with sixteen squares. The first one I made was with salvaged bits of an old sundress and blue jeans. I wasn't satisfied with the results because I knew I could do better. So I found a remnant of blue-and-white-striped fabric from the Roman blinds in my bedroom, cut sixteen more identical squares, and arranged them to look like a basket weave. But I really

wanted to impress my teacher, so I embroidered over every seam with a variety of stitches I found in a craft book. It was beautiful. And I got 100% on the assignment.

Crafting is in my genes. My mom is a very practical lady, and her craftiness was usually put to use for functional applications resulting from limited funds. She made her wedding dress, our Halloween costumes, and my high-school prom dress; she mended; and she knit mittens and afghans. She rarely made anything "just because." But everything she made was done beautifully and with love.

For me, it's all about the making, not the having. I'm always happy when I'm stitching and sewing, whether by hand or machine. I love having something to stitch when I'm watching TV or waiting for my girls while they're at extracurricular activities. I'll sit and stitch just about anywhere—family gatherings, piano lessons, dance class, gymnastics practice, airplanes, hotel rooms, and hospital waiting rooms ... my minivan ... seriously. That's one of my favorite things about embroidery, its portability. You can take it almost anywhere. If you're a stitcher, you're never bored.

And now, I love combining my love of quilting with embroidery. These two forms of needlework make a great partnership, and I loved designing the two embroidered quilts and fun little projects in this book.

INTRODUCTION

I'd like to say I designed these quilts for stitchers everywhere who are looking for the perfect embroidery designs to make for the cherished little ones in their lives. But I can't. The truth is the *… And Everything Nice* (page 44) quilt happened without intention. I designed it purely for fun while on an extended vacation with my family. I couldn't lug my sewing machine along with me, so I brought all my embroidery supplies instead.

I started fiddling around with a simple, embroidered tutu design. I wasn't sure what to do with it, but the little design was so pretty I started looking for a way to use it.

I don't remember how the alphabet got involved, but it did. And so did the nursery rhyme "What Are Little Girls Made Of?" Whenever I was stuck for an idea for a letter, I thought about little girls and pretty things. Sometimes I'd solicit advice from my daughters to help me come up with the perfect image, like the kitten and the words for the valentine. Next thing I knew, I had an entire alphabet of pretty little embroidery images.

But then I got to thinking about all the embroiderers who might enjoy making a boy version. I know if I had a boy and a girl I'd definitely need both patterns! *… And Puppy Dog Tails* quilt (page 80) just seemed a natural companion.

When it comes to a pleasing quilt design, the alphabet has, umm, an unfortunate number of letters. My not-so-original solution was to add a block to each corner. But what should be in them? A partial answer came during a conversation about personalizing a quilt, especially if it's a gift, and most especially if it's going to be a keepsake (which I guess all quilts should be, right?). So I put the "For" and "From" information—usually tucked away on the back—into the actual design. And wouldn't you know it, the lyrics of the alphabet song fit in the remaining blocks.

But my ideas shouldn't stop you from using your own creativity to stitch something original and personal to you. It took me a long time to realize that patterns aren't "laws" but suggestions, guidelines, or whatever you want them to be.

Nothing would make me happier than knowing my designs serve as inspiration for your own creativity, which takes you in a direction that makes you happy.

BASIC EMBROIDERY

You will notice that in this book I sometimes refer to my favorite or preferred method of doing things, and in some cases I won't commit to telling you the right or wrong way to do things. I've found that the element of personal preference is so important when it comes to satisfying one's creative spirit. Sometimes the same result can be accomplished in more than one way, and it often comes down to how you like to work. If you try something I suggest and it just doesn't work for you, try something else. Believe me, I've tried things that were recommended to me and I just didn't like, so I found another way that worked for me. And that has always helped me to really enjoy the process of embroidery—my way.

In this book I give you basic guidelines to get you started, but I encourage you to experiment with different methods and find your preferred ways of doing things.

EMBROIDERY FLOSS

All projects in this book are stitched with cotton six-ply floss.

Several brands of embroidery floss are available, and the price and quality vary. I've used many of them and have learned that you get what you pay for. Inexpensive floss tends to knot, twist, and misbehave, causing lots of frustration for the stitcher.

My favorite brand embroidery floss is Lecien's COSMO. All the embroidery in this book is stitched with COSMO floss. It handles nicely and stitches up beautifully.

Because DMC is also a very popular brand, all color-coded charts in this book refer to both COSMO and DMC embroidery floss. All flosses have numbers to identify their color. *Be aware that the numbers do not match from one brand to another.*

The floss colors indicated for each design were selected to match the fabrics I used for the quilts in this book.

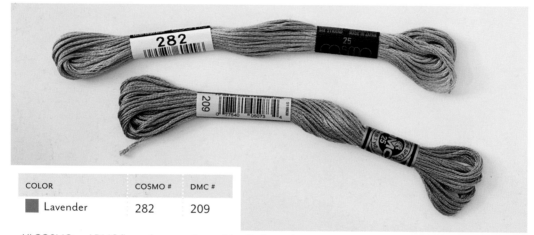

COLOR		COSMO #	DMC #
■	Lavender	282	209

All COSMO and DMC flosses have numbers to identify their color. Be aware that the numbers do not match from one brand to another.

COSMO brand 6-ply floss in colors used for ... And Everything Nice (page 44)

COSMO brand 6-ply floss in colors used for ... And Puppy Dog Tails (page 80)

But I understand that you probably won't get exactly the same fabrics I used. Or you may choose completely different colors for your projects. The embroidery police won't come and arrest you if you do. However, I strongly recommend choosing floss colors to coordinate with the fabrics you choose. I've included floss color swatches and descriptions for your reference. If you need help choosing floss colors to best go with your fabrics, an experienced salesperson at a good needlecraft or quilt store can help you.

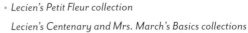

Lecien's Petit Fleur collection

Lecien's Centenary and Mrs. March's Basics collections

Tail end of the skein

Standard embroidery floss skein or hank

Tips for Working with Embroidery Floss

Here are a few tips for working with embroidery floss:

* Standard cotton six-ply embroidery floss is sold by the skein (sometimes called a hank).

* To start, look for the tail end—it is always located at the brand label end of the skein (not the bar code label end), regardless of the manufacturer—and gently pull until you have a length that's about 18˝–20˝ long (any longer and the floss will start to knot and fray). Cut off the length of floss.

* *Always* separate your plies before stitching. I used to skip this step. Now I know why my work didn't look as smooth and why the floss knotted.

Separate the plies.

* Here's a little trick to separating the plies. Hold one end of the length with two fingers, take one ply with the other hand, and gently pull the ply upward. Don't worry that the threads are collecting into a bunch under your fingers. They aren't getting tangled. As soon as the single ply is separated, the remaining plies will fall free and remain untangled.

Pull one ply from the top.

* For the projects in this book, I almost always use two plies for embroidery. Some design elements need only one ply and even fewer require three plies. The number of plies to use is noted in the projects.

SCISSORS

I'm a big believer in using the right tool for the job. When it comes to embroidery scissors, I favor spring-loaded thread snips. It's so easy to pick up the snips to cut without having to put your fingers through the holes of a regular pair of scissors. But that is just my personal preference. I also enjoy the aesthetic elegance and romance of small, decorated scissors designed especially for embroidery.

As long as your scissors are small and sharp, they will work.

I use small, sharp thread snips or scissors designed for embroidery.

NEEDLES

The function of an embroidery needle is to pierce a hole in the material big enough for the floss to comfortably pass through without too much friction. A good embroidery needle also has an eye that can accommodate up to six plies of embroidery floss and has a nice sharp tip. Any package of needles that specifies embroidery will be appropriate for the projects in this book.

Embroidery needles are available in different sizes (length and thickness). Many embroiderers develop a personal preference for one length. My favorite is size 10. If you are new to embroidery, buy a variety pack and try the different sizes until you find one that is most comfortable for you.

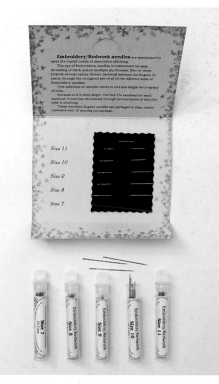

Jeana Kimball's Foxglove Cottage is my favorite brand of embroidery needles

THREADING A NEEDLE

To thread your needle, moisten the end of the plies, trim them on an angle with sharp embroidery scissors, and put the end through the eye of the needle.

KNOTTING THE FLOSS

A general belief seems to be that it's a serious offense to make knots on the back of your embroidery. I was taught to *never, ever* make a knot to start or finish a thread. I thought that was the one rule of embroidery that must never be broken. Why? Well, these are the two problems I've encountered:

* Knots can create lumps that may prevent the surface of framed embroidery from lying perfectly flat.

* A knot can cause problems when you try to make a stitch that shares the same or a nearby hole in the fabric. I've had my needle go through a knot, pulling it to the top of my work—very annoying.

Well, I guess I'm just "knotty" by nature—pardon the pun—because I use knots (almost) all the time.

Honestly, I can't be bothered with leaving a tail at the beginning. That just makes me cranky to have to go back, rethread the tail, and weave it into the stitches. (I can't figure out why I have lots of patience for some things and very little for others, but this is definitely a case of personal preference for me!)

Another starting method is to make a few overlapping backstitches to anchor the thread. But this really works only if you have stitches that are large enough to cover the backstitches, and because I rarely embroider "filled" designs, this method often doesn't work for me.

Weaving is another way to start and end a thread. This works only if you already have completed stitches through which to weave (or are willing to leave a tail). Sometimes I will weave my end tail back through my stitches, but I don't like carrying my thread long distances across the back. So depending on the design, this method may or may not work for me.

Knots are simply the fastest, easiest, and least fussy method of starting and ending my threads. That said, most of my embroidery is stitched into quilts, so lumping isn't usually an issue. Plus, my knots are on the small side. Oh, one final word on knots: If the embroidered piece will be subjected to wear and laundering, knotting both the beginning and the end of each embroidery thread will make your stitches more secure—they will be less likely to come undone while being enjoyed.

How I Knot the End of My Thread

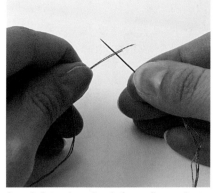

Step 1. *Point the tail end of your floss at the tip of your threaded needle.*

Step 2. *Hold the tail end against the needle and wrap the floss twice around the needle.*

Step 3. *Gently pinch the wraps between 2 fingers.*

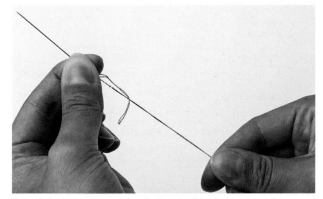

Step 4. *Slide the wraps down the length of the floss to the end. Vary the size of the knot with more or fewer wraps.*

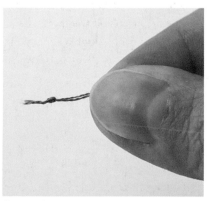

Knotted thread

So there you have it. I confess to being a rule breaker. It works for me, but now you have enough information to decide how you'd like to stitch.

FABRIC FOR STITCHING

Many beginners run to the safety of a solid white fabric, much like a painter often starts with a blank white canvas. Absolutely nothing is wrong with embroidering on a plain fabric. Nothing at all. There are examples of it in this book.

Solid colors

Plain white linen

But let me share a little secret with you. Choosing a fabric with a subtle, tonal print can enhance the beauty and interest of your embroidery significantly.

You will notice that most of the embroidery in this book is stitched on fabrics that, if you stand back and squint your eyes, look plain. The print isn't obvious enough to distract from hours of stitching. But up close, there is just enough detail in the background to add a layer of interest.

For example, I chose this stripe and ran it horizontally as a subtle reference to a road.

Horizontal stripes

Orienting the stripes vertically gives the design a very different look.

Vertical stripes

So when you're choosing fabric for your embroidery, consider something that is light enough to showcase your stitches but interesting enough to further delight both yourself and those who are lucky enough to enjoy your work up close.

Subtle tone-on-tone floral

Checks and dots

PREPARING YOUR FABRIC

Think about how the finished product will be used and laundered to help you decide if you should preshrink your fabrics before embroidering. Are you more likely to hand or machine wash? I suggest treating the unembroidered fabric or object (like clothing or home décor item) as you will after it's been embroidered. For example, a garment will definitely be washed, so follow the manufacturer's laundering instructions to wash and dry it before you stitch on it. Framed embroidery, especially if it is protected by glass, isn't likely to ever be washed.

Quilts and other objects are subject to more consideration if they have been embroidered. If the quilt will only be hung on a wall, you can decide if you want to preshrink your fabrics or not. But if the quilt will be washed, definitely preshrink your fabrics!

As a quilter I rarely preshrink my fabric, for three reasons: One, I can't be bothered with all the laundering and pressing. Two, when I get the urge or inspiration to make something, I don't want to wait; I just want to start cutting and sewing. And three, I prefer quilts that look well loved; so if I don't preshrink my fabrics, I can wash my finished quilt in warm water, throw it in the dryer on high, and have an instant family heirloom.

That said, I know many skilled and respected quilters who swear by preswashing for their own reasons.

Embroidery on baby garments

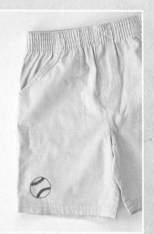
Embroidery on child's clothing

TRANSFERRING DESIGNS ONTO FABRIC

There are several ways to get an embroidery design onto fabric. This is my preferred method for drawing simple designs onto light quilter's cotton and other light fabrics.

I start by making a photocopy of the design and lightly taping it—right side up—to either a light box or a window. Windows are readily available, and even on a cloudy day you can get enough light to see the design through the fabric. The designs in this book are small and fairly quick to trace. But for bigger projects, tracing on a window can be hard on the arms. Light boxes range in price, size, and quality. I prefer them to windows because they're easier on my arms.

If you have a glass-top table, consider turning it into a makeshift light box by removing the shade from a desk lamp and placing the lamp underneath the glass.

Next, I center my fabric over the paper pattern and lightly tape it in place. Then I trace the design with my marker (see My Favorite Tracing Tool, page 22).

Center and tape fabric over photocopied pattern. Then trace the design.

Match the color of the pen to the thread.

Pigma Micron pens come in several colors.

MY FAVORITE TRACING TOOL

Embroidery markings fall into two categories, temporary and permanent. The word "permanent" used to stress me out because I didn't want any lines to show when my stitches weren't perfect or if the marked lines were thicker than the threads I used for stitching. But I've found a permanent method that works great for me—drawing solid or dotted lines using a Pigma Micron Pen. These pens are found in good art supply, craft, and some quilt stores, and they come in a range of basic colors. I try to match the pen color as closely to the floss color as I can to help hide any markings.

But if you just want to try one color that works well on white or light-colored fabric, go for brown (not to be confused with sepia, which is darker).

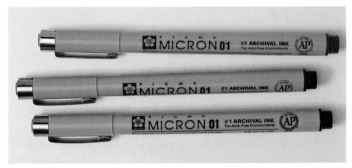

From top to bottom: brown, sepia, and black. I recommend brown for general tracing. The sepia and black are usually too dark and are more likely to show underneath stitches.

Pigma Micron Pens also come in different thicknesses. If you're a beginner or have somewhat uncooperative eyes, opt for the 05 size. But if you can handle a finer tip, my favorite is 01. I suggest taking a scrap of the fabric you plan to embroider on to the store and testing the different sizes to see which one you like best.

· · · **TIP** ·

When drawing lazy daisy stitches, just make a single dot to mark the top and bottom of each petal.

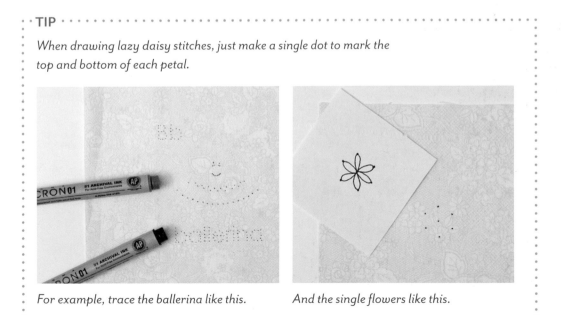

For example, trace the ballerina like this.　　　*And the single flowers like this.*

A few cautionary words about temporary markers: Yes, the concept is appealing. But it's best to trace the entire design before you start stitching, and temporary markers aren't always cooperative.

For example, some temporary fabric markers are heat sensitive and are easily removed with a hot iron. Sounds great, right? But if you like to press your work as you go, before you've finished all the stitching, your unstitched marks will disappear, forcing you to retrace. Or sometimes a piece of embroidery gets shoved unceremoniously somewhere (not that I'd know anything about that!). If it isn't rescued right away, deep creases could form that will make it difficult to stitch accurately, so pressing is required before you continue.

This situation is not ideal because as soon as you stitch on your fabric, it becomes slightly distorted and the bulk of the thread can make it very difficult to retrace the design accurately.

Other temporary markers wash out (supposedly), but humidity can cause the marks to disappear before you want them to. Also, some are supposed to disappear on their own after a period of time. But if you take longer than you planned to finish your stitching, again you're forced to retrace.

I've also known the pain of using a washable pen that didn't live up to its promise, so I advise caution with so-called washable fabric markers.

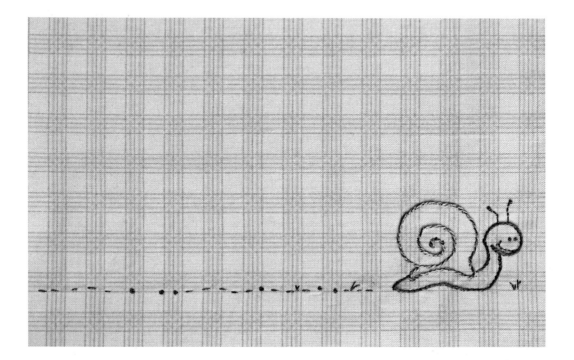

4˝ wooden hoop with adjustable screw

HOOPS

To hoop or not to hoop, that is the question.

I was taught to always use a hoop because it helps avoid tension problems.

I grew up fearing the hoopless approach and never tried it …

… until one day it occurred to me while cross-stitching that I could go twice as fast if I got rid of the hoop. Instead of doing a single pull of the needle and floss every time I passed the needle through the fabric (a down stitch or an up stitch—known as a stab stitch), I could do a continuous "down–up" stitch. My productivity doubled and I was one happy stitcher.

When I returned to embroidery I was very comfortable stitching continuous stitches without a hoop. And to my surprise, I didn't have any tension problems.

Now here's a qualification. Embroidery stitches can, for the most part, be classified as one of two types of stitches: stab or continuous.

Continuous Stitches

Stitches that are completed by passing the needle from front to back to front in one movement are continuous stitches. For example, a stem stitch or backstitch is completed with a down-up movement of the needle before pulling the floss through the fabric.

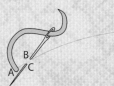

A stem stitch is considered a continuous stitch because it is completed with one pass of the needle through the fabric in both directions.

Stab Stitches

Stitches made by passing the needle completely through the fabric in one direction at a time are stab stitches. For example, colonial knots and the satin stitch are made by pulling the needle through to the top side of your fabric and then pushing the needle through the fabric to the back. In other words, two stabs equal one completed stitch.

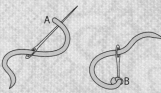

Two passes through the fabric with a needle are required to complete a colonial knot.

I'm comfortable with or without a hoop for continuous stitches but tend to favor without because I can control my stitches better and it's just more comfortable for my hand. But some stitchers prefer to hold a hoop rather than limp cloth.

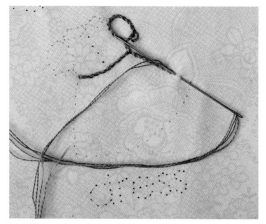

I don't use a hoop for continuous stitches.

I do use a hoop for stab stitches because I need another hand to stabilize my fabric while I'm wrapping floss around the needle for knots and for aiming my needle accurately.

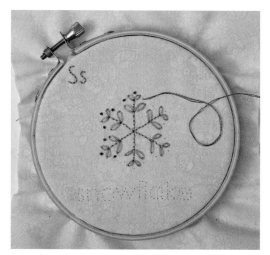

I use a hoop for stab stitches.

When I use a hoop, I've found that a smaller hoop, 4˝ diameter, is more comfortable for my hand. (But I have little fingers so you might prefer something slightly larger.) Contrary to popular belief, the size of an embroidery hoop is more relevant to the size of your hand, *not* the size of the design you are stitching.

I also wrap a strip of muslin around the inner hoop to make it a little gentler on my fabric.

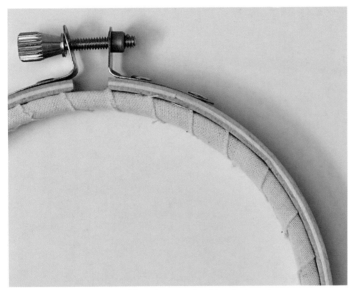

I wrap the inner ring with a ¾˝-wide strip of unbleached muslin.

One last thing about hoops: If you do use one, get into the habit of taking your work out of the hoop when you set it down for the day. The longer cloth sits in a hoop, the greater the likelihood of the fabric becoming distorted. You may have the best intentions of picking up your embroidery the next day, but sometimes days turn into weeks, weeks turn into months ... you know where this is going, right? I once left a piece of work in a hoop for several months (a year maybe?), and the metal oxidized and stained the fabric. If you've got one of those sitting around, do me a favor, and throw it out!

BACKING

Embroidery backing can be muslin, interfacing, or some other fabric stabilizer used to line the back of the fabric before you start embroidering. Two reasons to use backing for your embroidery are—

One: To make the fabric less transparent—so the floss on the back won't show through and cause unsightly shadowing, especially on lighter fabric

Two: To provide additional stability to the fabric, so it won't distort or pucker as you stitch

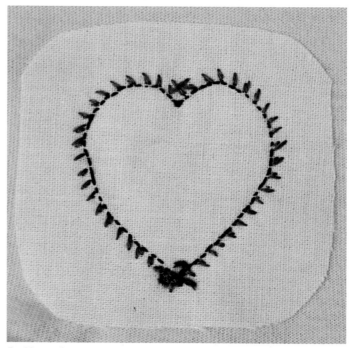

Fusible interfacing on the back of a jersey-knit garment

However, backing is another aspect of embroidery where I don't have a right or wrong answer. I've stitched both ways and with only a few exceptions (such as stitching on jersey-knit), I prefer to embroider without backing. I almost always stitch on white or very light cotton fabric, but I don't carry my floss across the back very far, so I've never had a problem with shadowing.

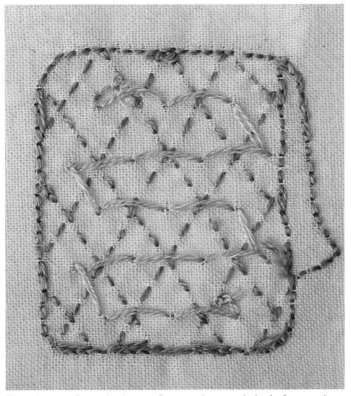

Thread carry refers to the distance floss travels across the back of your embroidery from the end of one stitch to the beginning of the next stitch, as shown by the blue floss.

It is surprisingly easy to regulate your tension without a hoop; you're not trying to cinch Scarlett O'Hara's corset for heaven's sake! The cotton fabrics I choose—usually 100% quilting cotton—are stable enough for my purposes, so I've never finished a piece of embroidery and then wished I'd lined it. (I did once use a fusible interfacing that puckered horribly when my stitching was done ... live and learn, but *always* test!)

Again, however, many experienced and highly regarded embroiderers swear by backing. You may want to experiment with them, especially as there are new embroidery backing products on the market that I've never tried.

TRIMMING EMBROIDERED BLOCKS

Most of the embroidered blocks in this book are trimmed to an unfinished size of 4˝ × 4˝. Whether they are sewn into a quilt, nine-patch pillow, or stuffed toy block, they measure 3½˝ × 3½˝ finished.

Although a 4˝ × 4˝ ruler isn't necessary to trim your blocks accurately, I strongly recommend using one. It makes the job go much quicker and practically eliminates measuring/cutting errors on your precious handwork.

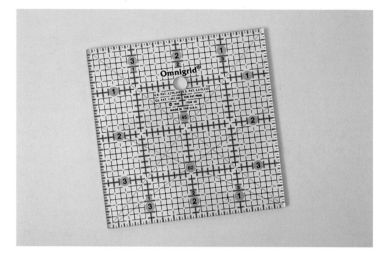

When you trace the embroidery design onto your blocks, mark a dot in each corner to create your trim lines.

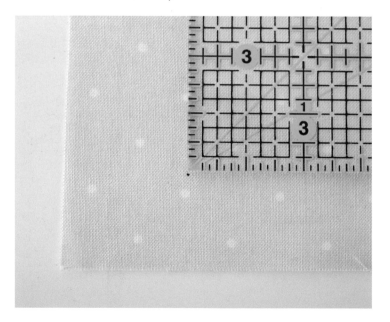

When you've finished embroidering a block, lay it on a self-healing mat and line up the corners of the 4″ ruler with the four dots as best you can. Embroidery will always cause at least a little distortion of your fabric—that's normal. Don't worry if your ruler corners don't match the dots exactly. (Mine never do!)

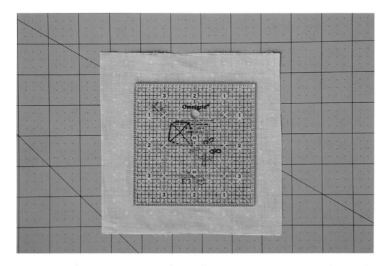

You can center the ruler from left to right and top to bottom and then easily trim all four sides of the block without moving the ruler.

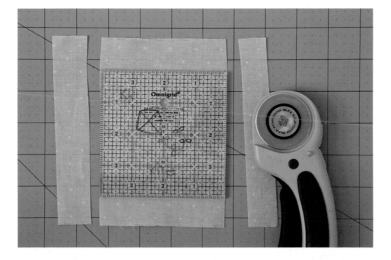

EMBROIDERY STITCH GUIDE

MY FAVORITE STITCH ...

... is the stem (or outline) stitch, and it's the one I used for most of the designs in this book. I'm a fan of the stem stitch for a few reasons:

* The lines created with this stitch are a little thicker than the also-popular backstitch.

* It has a nice texture that looks like a twisted rope.

* If you have trouble achieving a consistent backstitch length (as I do), this stitch can help camouflage that little imperfection.

The stem and outline stitches are basically the same except for the position of the thread. I almost always refer to both stitches as stem stitch out of habit, but I use the abbreviation OS for both stitches to keep them from being confused with SS for the satin stitch.

When stitching a straight line, it doesn't really matter if you use the stem stitch or the outline stitch. When stitching a curved line, however, I always make sure the thread goes to the outside edge of the curve.

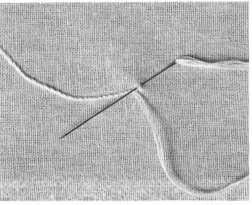

Stem stitch—thread lays below the needle

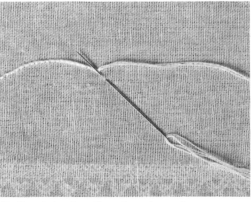

Outline stitch —thread lays above the needle

To give the letters and words in each design a nice crisp finish, I stitched them with a backstitch using two plies of floss. But because the stem stitch is my favorite "drawing" stitch, I used it for most of the design work. Sometimes I used the backstitch for details and elements I wanted to appear smaller.

If you really love the backstitch or really dislike the stem stitch, all the projects in this book will look just as lovely if you replace all the stem or outline stitches with the backstitch.

MY FAVORITE KNOT

... is *not* the French knot—even though it is arguably the most common embroidery knot. It's easy to teach and easy to make, but it's also easy to vary the size of this knot with the number of times the thread is wrapped around the needle.

I don't know if it's just me, but I get all kinds of tangles and messes when I'm making French knots and often have to cut my thread, cut out all my knots, and start again. It's very frustrating for me. In fact, I haven't made one since I discovered **the colonial knot**.

Colonial knot

The colonial knot is lovely. After you get the hang of the figure-8 wrap around the needle, it goes just as quickly as the French knot. It doesn't misbehave for me, and it lies nice and flat on the surface of my embroidery—unlike the French knot, which sticks up higher.

If you're not familiar with the colonial knot, I highly recommend giving it a try! I've taught this knot in many classes, and after people get the hang of it, they never go back.

But in case you're a French knot fan or you don't like the colonial knot, the instructions for both knots are here and they are interchangeable for every design in the book.

Stitches

Backstitch (BS)

Chain Stitch (CS)

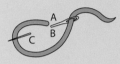

Colonial Knot (CK)

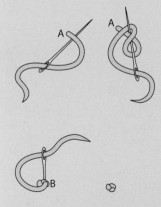

Couching (C)

Open Lazy Daisy Stitch (OLD)

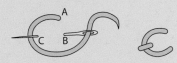

French Knot (FK)

Running Stitch (RS)

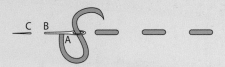

Fly Stitch (FS)

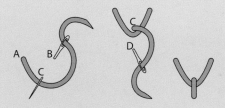

Satin Stitch (SS)

Lazy Daisy Stitch (LD)

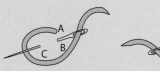

Outline or Stem Stitch (OS)

Straight Stitch (TS)

Aa — ant
Bb — baseball
Cc — car
Next time won't you sing with me?

Ee — energy
Ff — fort
Gg — goal
Hh — hammer

Jj — jacks
Kk — kite
Ll — ladder
Mm — mask

Oo — octopus
Pp — puppy
Qq — quarter
Rr — robot

Tt — tornado
Uu — up
Vv — volcano
Ww — web

Xx — X marks the spot
Yy — yo-yo
Zz — zzz ...
For my darling boy

BASIC QUILTING
INSTRUCTIONS

If you're new to quilting, this book won't teach you everything you need to know, but here are a few basic instructions to help you put together an alphabet quilt.

STANDARD TOOLS

Two of the best inventions, in my opinion, are the rotary cutter and the self-healing mat. Together with a quilting ruler, these tools have revolutionized quilting.

Rotary Cutter

A rotary cutter is a tool with a sharp, circular blade that rolls like a wheel when you move it across a cutting surface.

Self-Healing Mat

Because a rotary cutter is very sharp, it will either damage most surfaces with its blade or dull very quickly if used on a hard surface. The self-healing mat was designed to be hard enough to support the sharpness of the rotary blade, but soft enough to not dull the cutting edge. Several sizes are available. A good standard size is 18˝ × 24˝.

Ruler

Quilting rulers come in many different sizes. Most are conveniently marked with ⅛˝ grids to help you cut fabric with accuracy. If you're only going to buy one ruler, I recommend the 6½˝ × 24˝.

For most of the projects in this book, I also strongly recommend a 4˝ × 4˝ square ruler (see Trimming Embroidered Blocks, pages 30–33).

SEAM ALLOWANCES

A ¼˝ seam allowance is used for most of the sewn projects. It's a good idea to do a test seam before you begin sewing to check that your ¼˝ is accurate.

PRESSING

In general, press seams toward the darker fabric. In some cases, I recommend pressing seams open. Press lightly in an up-and-down motion; do not push or pull the iron across the fabric. Avoid using a very hot iron or ironing too much, which can distort shapes and blocks. Be especially careful when pressing the bias edges of triangles because they stretch easily.

When you press your embroidery, lay a pressing cloth, such as a few layers of flannel, on your ironing surface and then place your embroidery right side down on the cloth. The stitches will nest into the soft surface underneath and won't get crushed.

BORDERS

When you've finished the quilt top patchwork and are ready to add the borders, measure the top through the center vertically. Cut the side borders this length, and mark the center points on each. Mark the center points of the sides of the quilt top with pins. Pin the side borders to the quilt top, matching the center pins. Using a ¼˝ seam allowance, sew the borders to the quilt top and press toward the border.

Then, measure horizontally across the center of the quilt top. Cut the top and bottom borders this length. Repeat for the top and bottom as described above, pinning, sewing, and pressing.

BATTING

The type of batting to use is a personal decision. If you're unsure what to use, consult your local quilt shop. I prefer a low loft (thinner) batting made with natural fibers like cotton. Bamboo batting has been available for a few years and it is lovely. My absolute favorite is silk batting; it is so easy to work with and drapes beautifully. But it's also a little on the pricey side.

LAYERING

Layering is the process of putting your quilt top, batting, and backing fabric all together. This is often called a "quilt sandwich."

Spread out the backing, wrong side up, and tape the edges down with masking tape. (If you are working on carpet, you can use T-pins to secure the backing to the carpet.) Center the batting on top, smoothing out any folds. Center the quilt top, right side up, on top of the batting and backing.

BASTING

Basting keeps the quilt layers from shifting while you are quilting.

If you plan to machine quilt, pin baste the quilt layers together with safety pins placed about 3˝–4˝ apart. Baste vertical and then horizontal rows, working from the center out to the edges. Try not to pin directly where you intend to quilt.

If you plan to hand quilt, baste the layers together with thread using a long needle and light-colored thread. Knot one end of the thread. Using stitches approximately the length of the needle, baste vertical and then horizontal rows about 4˝ apart, working from the center out to the edges. Add two diagonal rows of basting from corner to corner.

QUILTING

Quilting, also known as topstitching, whether by hand or machine, enhances the pieced or appliquéd design of the quilt. You may choose to quilt in-the-ditch, echo the pieced or appliqué motifs, use patterns from quilting design books and stencils, or do your own free-motion quilting.

Entire books are dedicated to this subject ... way too much information for me to cover here. If you'd like to learn more about topstitching, ask at your local quilt shop for book recommendations.

After the quilting is finished, trim the edges of your quilt to remove the excess batting and to straighten the edges in preparation for the next step—binding.

BINDING

Piece the binding strips together with diagonal seams to make a continuous binding strip. Trim the seam allowance to ¼˝. Press the seams open.

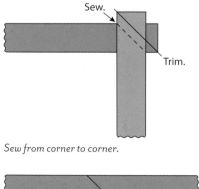

Sew from corner to corner.

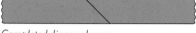

Completed diagonal seam

Press the entire strip in half lengthwise with wrong sides together. Next, with raw edges even, pin the binding to the front of the quilt. (I usually start in the middle of the bottom edge.) Leave the first few inches of the binding unattached. Pin up to a few inches away from a corner. Sew the binding to the quilt, using a ¼˝ seam allowance.

Stop sewing ¼˝ away from the first corner and backstitch one or two stitches (see Step 1). Lift the presser foot and needle. Rotate the quilt one-quarter turn. Fold the binding at a right angle so it extends straight above the quilt and the fold forms a 45° angle in the corner (see Step 2). Then bring the binding strip down even with the edge of the quilt (see Step 3). Begin sewing at the folded edge. Repeat in the same manner at all corners.

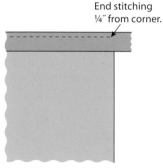

Step 1. *Stitch to ¼˝ from corner.*

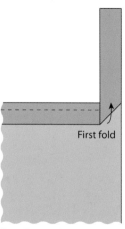

Step 2. *First fold for miter*

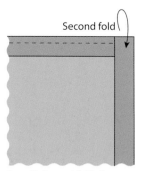

Step 3. *Second fold alignment*

Continue stitching until you are back near the beginning of the binding strip. To join the ends of the binding, fold the ending tail of the binding back on itself where it meets the beginning binding tail. From the fold, measure and mark the cut width of your binding strip. Cut the ending binding tail to this measurement. For example, if the binding is cut 2˝ wide, measure from the fold on the ending tail of the binding 2˝, and cut the binding tail to this length.

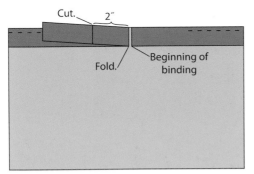

Cut binding tail.

Open both tails. Place one tail on top of the other tail at right angles, right sides together. Mark a diagonal line from corner to corner and stitch on the line. Check that you've done it correctly and that the binding fits the quilt; then trim the seam allowance to ¼˝. Press open.

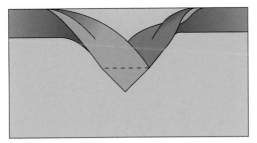

Stitch ends of binding diagonally.

Refold the binding and stitch this binding section in place on the quilt. Fold the binding over the raw edges to the quilt back and hand stitch.

... And Everything Nice Quilt

Finished size: 32½˝ × 37¾˝

YOU WILL NEED

COLOR	QUANTITY	COSMO #	DMC #
Brown, dark	1 skein	369	3790
Brown, medium	2 skeins	367	3032
Brown, light	1 skein	366	3782
Purple, medium	1 skein	282	209
Blue, dark	1 skein	214	334
Blue, medium	1 skein	2212	3755
Blue-green, light	1 skein	563	598
Green, medium	1 skein	2317	368
Yellow, medium	1 skein	701	3820
Pink, dark	1 skein	483	961
Pink, medium	1 skein	482	3716
Pink, light	1 skein	481	962
Gray, dark	1 skein	893	169
Gray, medium	1 skein	891	648
Gray, very light or Snow white	1 skein	*151 or *2500	*762 or *B5200

> **• • • NOTE • • • •**
>
> *Mix and match the embroidery designs from this project with the designs from ... And Puppy Dog Tails (beginning on page 80) to customize the quilt for your special child. The settings are interchangeable, too.*

*You don't need both pearl gray and snow white. This color is used to stitch drop pearls in the T is for Tiara block. If you're stitching on white fabric, use a light or very light pearl gray embroidery floss so it will be seen on the white background. If you're stitching on a darker fabric, use white or very white embroidery floss. (Yes, white embroidery floss comes in several shades!)

> **• • NOTE • • •**
>
> *A 4˝ square ruler is very helpful for trimming the embroidery squares.*

* 1¼ yards (1.1 meters) of background fabric for embroidery blocks and posts

* 1½ yards total (1.4 meters) of assorted prints or a 9˝ square each of 30 different prints

* ¼ yard (0.15 meter) for inner border

* ⅜ yard (0.35 meter) for outer border

* 1¼ yards (1.1 meters) for backing

* ⅓ yard (0.3 meter) for binding

* 37˝ × 42˝ piece of quilt batting (crib size)

CUTTING

Background

* 30 squares 6˝ × 6˝ for embroidered blocks, trimmed to 4˝ after embroidering

* 42 squares 2¼˝ × 2¼˝ for posts

Assorted prints

* 142 squares 2⅝˝ × 2⅝˝ (or 5 each of 30 fabrics) for half-square triangles

Inner border

4 strips 1˝ × fabric width

Outer border

4 strips 2¼˝ × fabric width

Binding

4 strips 2˝ × fabric width

Embroidered Blocks

Complete the embroidery on all 30 alphabet blocks using the Embroidered Blocks for ... *And Everything Nice* (pages 50–79). Use 2 plies of floss unless otherwise stated. Use medium brown floss and the backstitch for the alphabet letters and words. Trim each embroidered square to 4˝ × 4˝ (see Trimming Embroidered Blocks, pages 30–33).

Trace the design onto the 2¼˝ post squares (page 49) but wait until the quilt top is assembled to stitch the flowers.

Half-Square Triangle Units

1. On the wrong side of 71 assorted print squares, use a pencil and ruler to draw a diagonal line.

2. Randomly pair a marked square with an unmarked square, right sides together. Sew a scant ¼˝ seam on both sides of the pencil line.

3. Cut on the pencil line.

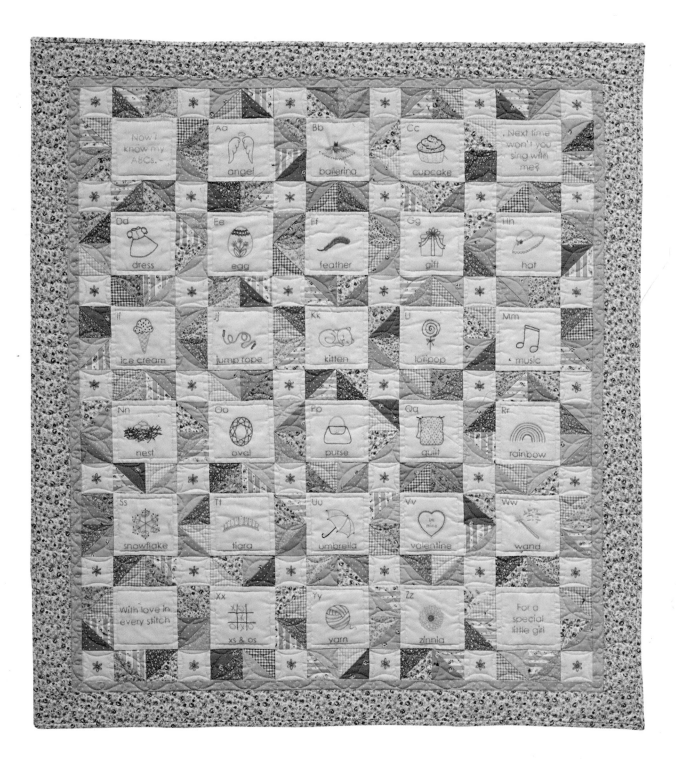

4. Press the seam toward the darker fabric and trim off the dog ears.

5. Measure the first unit for accuracy; it should be 2¼˝ × 2¼˝. Adjust the width of your seam allowance, if necessary, to achieve a perfect 2¼˝ × 2¼˝ unit.

6. Repeat Steps 2–5 to make 142 units.

7. Randomly pair up 2 half-square triangle units and sew them together, paying attention to the direction of the triangle seams.

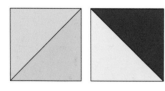

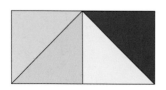

8. Measure the first unit for accuracy; it should be 2¼˝ × 4˝. Adjust the width of your seam allowance, if necessary, to achieve a perfect 2¼˝ × 4˝ unit.

9. Make 71 units.

10. Press the seam open.

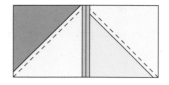

Construction

1. Sew together 5 random half-square triangle units and 6 posts (2¼˝ × 2¼˝ squares). Pay attention to the direction of the diagonal seams; the orientation alternates. Make 7 rows.

2. Lay out the embroidered blocks and the half-square triangle units in rows. Watch the orientation of the diagonal seams on the half-square triangle units very carefully. Be sure the blocks are in the correct order. Sew the blocks and units into rows. Make 6 rows.

3. Lay out the post rows between the embroidered block rows.

> **· · NOTE ·**
>
> *Be sure every other post row is rotated 180°.*

4. Sew the rows together.

5. Stitch the embroidered flowers to the posts.

Borders

1. Trim the inner borders and add them to the quilt top as shown in Borders (page 40).

2. Trim the outer borders and add them to the quilt top as shown in Borders (page 40).

Finishing

Layer, baste, quilt as desired, and bind (pages 41–43).

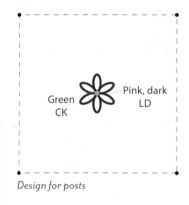

Green CK   Pink, dark LD

Design for posts

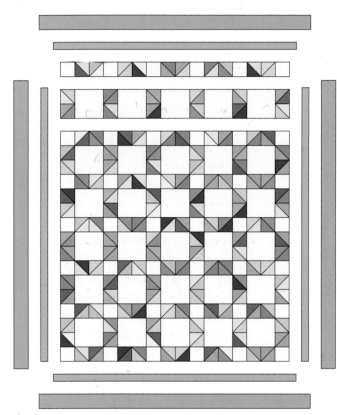

Quilt construction

... And Everything Nice

A is for Angel

The gently overlapping curves suggest the softness of feathers, and the wings look elegant with pointed tips. It would be nice to make the halo with a metallic or sparkly thread.

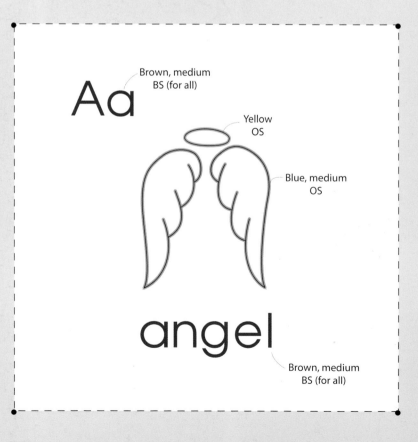

B is for Ballerina

I love how the elongated lazy daisy stitches create the feel of a tulle pouf on the ballet tutu. The knots along the bottom are little jewels that frame the skirt perfectly.

B

Bb

Pink, dark
SS

Pink, medium
LD

Pink, light
LD

Pink, medium
CK

ballerina

C is for Cupcake

I like how the little straight stitches look like "jimmies" sprinkled on this cupcake. They add so much color and festivity to this little confection. Knots would also be very charming. Choose the colors you want. The vertical running stitches are a subtle detail that creates the paper cupcake wrapper. A solid line would look too much like a stripe.

Cc

1 ply each
Brown, medium & dark
OS

Brown, light
OS/RS

cupcake

D is for Dress

I have always loved the classic Peter Pan collar. And little puffy sleeves with a cuff are pleasing details to look at and to stitch. I left the skirt blank, but it's a perfect opportunity to personalize or embellish.

D

Dd

Pink, dark
OS/TS

Blue green
CK

dress

E is for Egg

This happy egg is one of my favorite designs in this book. The flowers are the perfect sign of spring, and the lacy scallop trim finishes the top of the egg very nicely.

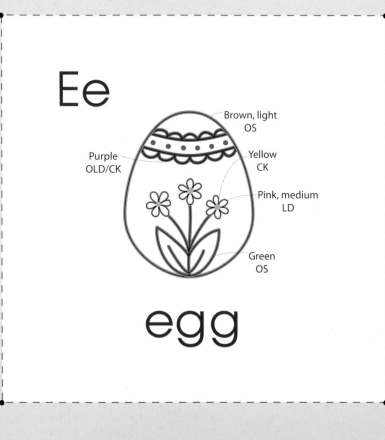

F is for Feather

Interestingly, the middle line of the feather is created not with stitches but by the seam where the many stitches meet. And subtle texture is created by very slightly staggering the length of the stitches along the outside edge of the feather.

F

Ff

Brown, medium
TS

Brown, dark
OS

feather

G is for Gift

Paying attention to even little dimensional elements can enhance the effectiveness of a design. The ribbon wrapping underneath the box looks more realistic because it is not perfectly lined up with the bottom edge of the box. And by extending the ribbon tails beyond the box, even more depth is created.

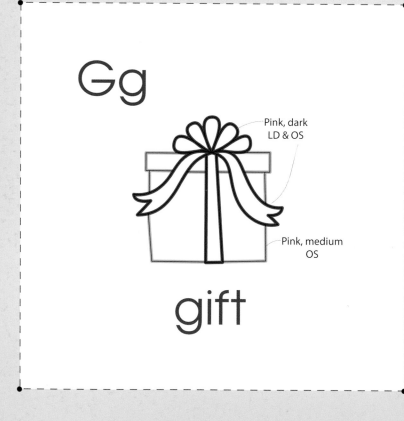

Gg

Pink, dark
LD & OS

Pink, medium
OS

gift

H is for Hat

Color plays an important role here. Stitching the hat in yellow is a clear reference to straw, a favorite material for summer bonnets. The open lazy daisy stitches along the bottom are very delicate, but they create a pretty lace trim.

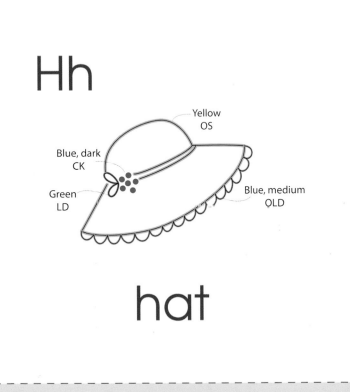

Hh

Yellow
OS

Blue, dark
CK

Green
LD

Blue, medium
OLD

hat

I is for Ice Cream

I thought little knots with a single ply of floss to make chocolate chips would be fun and add interest. Two plies of floss would make the chips too big. Consider changing the color to depict a different flavor!

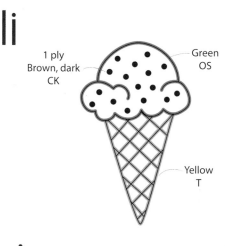

Ii

1 ply
Brown, dark
CK

Green
OS

Yellow
T

ice cream

J is for Jump Rope

Simple stitches can add amazing texture. This single, curved chain stitch makes the rope look more realistic.

J

Jj

Brown, light
CS

Blue, dark
OS

jump rope

K is for Kitten

I made this sleeping kitten look soft with both the color and the gently curved lines. And the very tiny bit of pink for the nose and mouth adds to the sweetness of this peaceful creature.

Kk

Gray, medium
OS

Pink, medium
BS

kitten

L is for Lollipop

In my mind, the perfect lollipop is made with more than one color. Creating this twisted look is easy with 2 plies of color and 1 ply of white. Most embroidery stitches look best when the strands are kept untwisted. But to achieve the effect in this lollipop, you must force the 3 plies to twist a lot while you make each stitch.

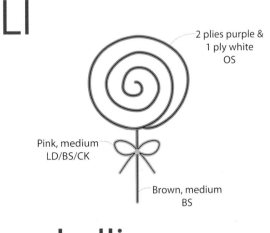

Ll

2 plies purple &
1 ply white
OS

Pink, medium
LD/BS/CK

Brown, medium
BS

lollipop

M is for Music

Even though technically the circles of these notes should be filled in, I left them open to keep this design from looking too heavy and dark. Call it creative license!

Gray, dark
OS

N is for Nest

I wanted to give the twigs and branches a somewhat realistic appearance. By using 2 similar-but-different browns together I created additional texture in the nest. Groups of 3 are pleasing to the eye, so I put 3 eggs in this nest.

N

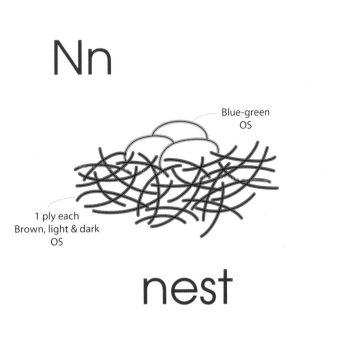

Nn

Blue-green
OS

1 ply each
Brown, light & dark
OS

nest

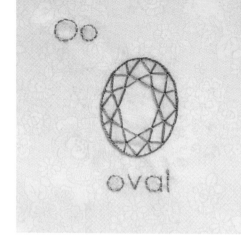

O is for Oval

The facets of this jewel are made with only one straight stitch for each clean line. The design is very simple and the straight lines are effective. Only the outside edge is done with a stem stitch to create a smooth, curved line.

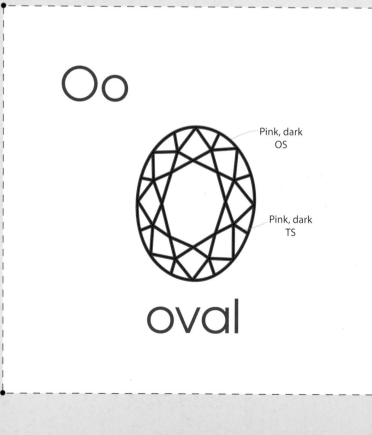

Oo

Pink, dark
OS

Pink, dark
TS

oval

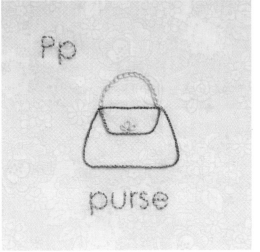

P is for Purse

For the letter J, I used the chain stitch to create a jump rope. Here, I used the same stitch to create a metal chain for the purse handle. And the lazy daisy stitch is perfect for making a metal clasp.

P

Pp

Yellow
CS

Yellow
LD

Blue, dark
US

purse

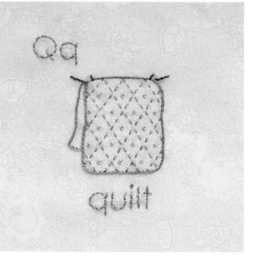

Q is for Quilt

This design is immediately recognizable as a quilt without any reference to patchwork; a simple diamond grid made with a running stitch is all the suggestion needed. The colonial knots add a little bit of color. By hanging the quilt on a clothesline and curling one corner, this image has life and interest.

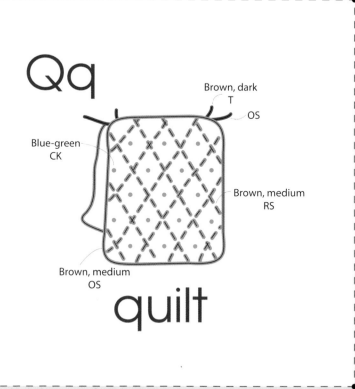

Qq

Brown, dark
T
OS

Blue-green
CK

Brown, medium
RS

Brown, medium
OS

quilt

R is for Rainbow

This rainbow is the perfect opportunity to make a block with (almost) all the colors of floss used in the quilt, which gives a nice balance to some of the less-colorful neighboring blocks.

R

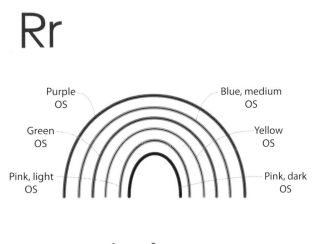

Rr

Purple
OS

Blue, medium
OS

Green
OS

Yellow
OS

Pink, light
OS

Pink, dark
OS

rainbow

S is for Snowflake

This otherwise sharp and icy element of nature is made to look soft with the gentle curves of the lazy daisy stitches and colonial knots that float around the edges. The knots do not need to be attached to the flake to be understood as part of the crystal.

Blue, dark
CK

Blue, medium
LD/BS

snowflake

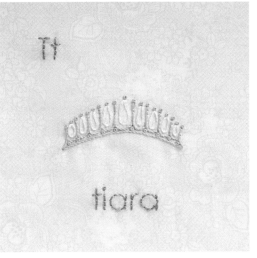

T is for Tiara

I wanted this delicate yet impressive headpiece to look more realistic than toylike. The use of yellow and either white or gray is effective in replicating the look of gold metal and tear-drop pearls. The colonial knot at the top of each pearl adds an element of filigree without making the tiara appear too heavy or gaudy.

T

Tt

Gray, light
or
White
LD

Yellow
CK

Yellow
OS

tiara

U is for Umbrella

This umbrella could have been oriented in many different positions. I like the way it appears to be resting on the floor as a child would put it after coming in from the rain.

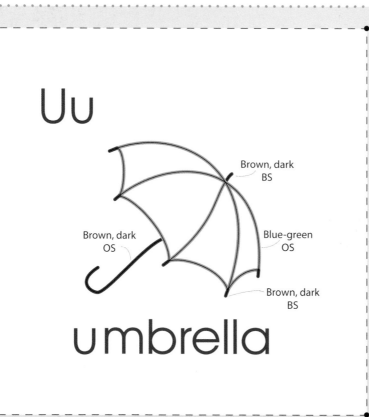

Uu

Brown, dark
BS

Blue-green
OS

Brown, dark
OS

Brown, dark
BS

umbrella

V is for Valentine

I repeated my trick used in H is for Hat, creating a delicate lace by using an open lazy daisy stitch. The love message is backstitched with a single ply because the words are very tiny. You can personalize the message.

Vv

Pink, light
OLD

be
mine

1 ply
Purple
BS

Pink, dark
OS

valentine

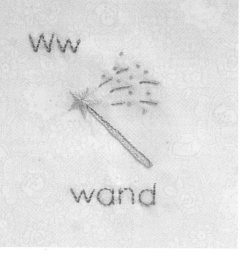

W is for Wand

This wand has the appearance of movement from the trail of lines and sparkles. I like how it looks as if it is casting a spell at this very moment. As with the angel's halo, a sparkly thread would be perfect to use here.

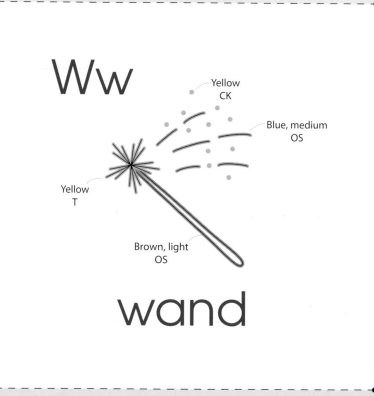

Ww

Yellow
CK

Blue, medium
OS

Yellow
T

Brown, light
OS

wand

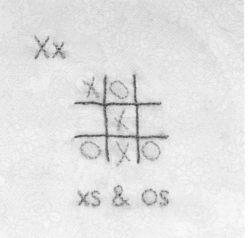

X is for Xs and Os

To make this design, I drew the game board and asked my daughters to play. I stopped them before anyone won or lost. Adding personal touches like this to your embroidery makes it very special. It also gives a somewhat naïve quality to the design.

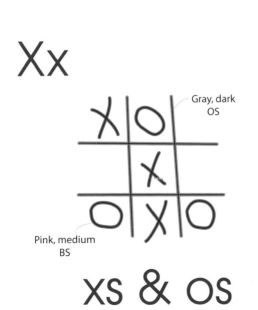

Gray, dark
OS

Pink, medium
BS

Y is for Yarn

I don't knit, but my mom does. My daughters have enjoyed years of handmade mittens, sweaters, and hats, courtesy of Grandma's knitting needles, just as I did growing up.

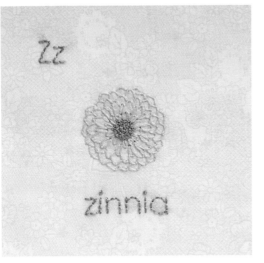

Z is for Zinnia

The lazy daisy stitches—both open and closed—are effective in creating the tiny petals of this flower that are layered in rounds. And the tight cluster of colonial knots in the center adds additional texture.

Zz

Yellow
LD/OLD

Green
CK

zinnia

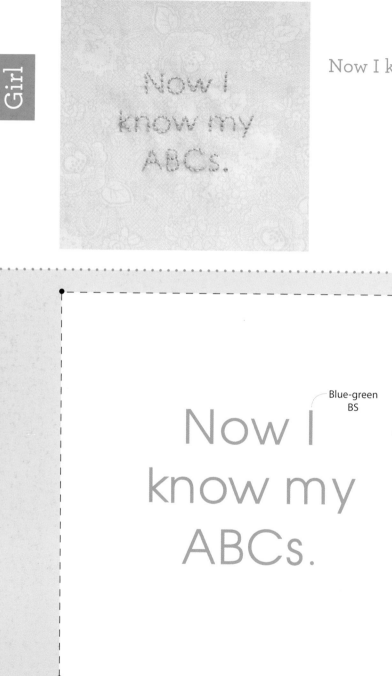

Now I know my ABCs

Now I
know my
ABCs.

Blue-green
BS

Next time won't you
sing with me?

Next time
won't you
sing with
me?

Pink, medium
BS

With love in every stitch

Purple
BS

With love in
every stitch

For a special little girl

For a
special
little girl

Blue, medium
BS

is for Stitch

... And Puppy Dog Tails Quilt

Finished size: 34˝ × 39½˝

YOU WILL NEED

COLOR	QUANTITY	COSMO #	DMC #
Brown, medium	2 skeins	368	3790
Red, medium	1 skein	466	3777
Orange, medium	1 skein	186	976
Yellow, medium	1 skein	2702	3827
Green, dark	1 skein	925	936
Blue, dark	1 skein	735	924
Blue, medium	1 skein	733	926
Gray, dark	1 skein	155	3799
Gray, medium	1 skein	894	3022
Gray, light	1 skein	892	3023
Brown, dark	1 skein	369	3781
Brown, light	1 skein	367	3032

· · · NOTE · · · · · · ·

Mix and match the embroidery designs from this project with the designs from ... And Everything Nice (page 44) to customize the quilt for your special child. The settings are interchangeable, too.

* 1 yard (0.8 meter) of background fabric for embroidery blocks

* 1½ yards total (1.4 meters) of assorted prints or a 9˝ square each of 30 different prints

* ¼ yard (0.15 meter) for inner border

* ⅜ yard (0.35 meter) for outer border

* 1¼ yards (1.1 meters) for backing

* ⅜ yard (0.35 meter) for binding

* 38˝ × 44˝ piece of quilt batting

Embroidered Blocks

Complete the embroidery on all 30 alphabet blocks using the Embroidered Blocks for ... *And Puppy Dog Tails* (pages 86–115). Use 2 plies of floss unless otherwise stated. Use medium brown floss and the backstitch for the alphabet letters and words. Trim each embroidered square to 4˝ × 4˝ (see Trimming Embroidered Blocks, pages 30–33).

Pieced Blocks

Before adding frames to the embroidered squares, decide if you want a controlled or scrappy look to the quilt. For a controlled look, frame each square with 4 rectangles of the same fabric. For a scrappy look, frame each square with 4 random fabric rectangles.

1. Choose 4 frame rectangles.

2. With right sides together, align the first rectangle along the right edge of the embroidered block. Starting at the top, sew a seam about halfway along the edge (Figure 1). Press the seam away from the embroidered block.

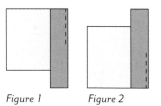

Figure 1   Figure 2

> **IMPORTANT**
>
> *To ensure all the blocks are framed exactly the same way, always line up the short edge of the first rectangle with the top edge of the block as shown in Figure 1, not the bottom edge as shown in Figure 2.*

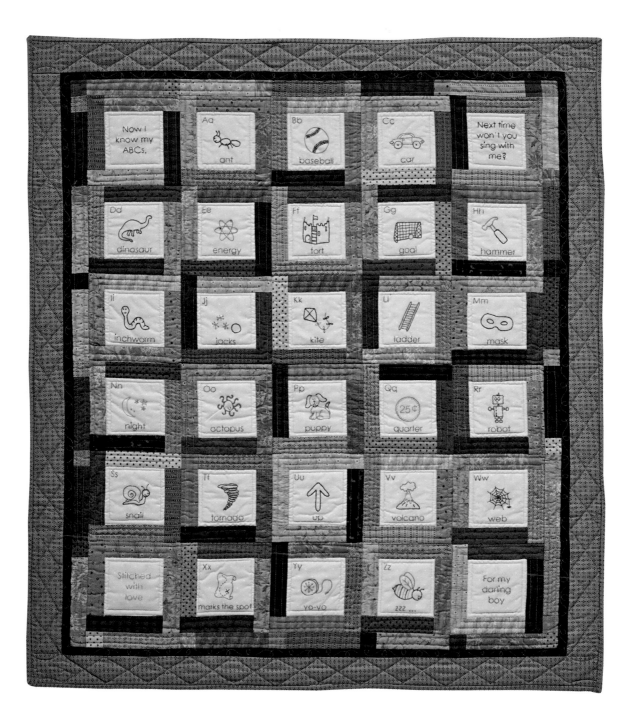

3. With right sides together, align the second rectangle along the top edge of the embroidered block. Sew the entire seam (Figure 3). Press the seam away from the embroidered block.

Figure 3

4. Repeat for the remaining 2 rectangles (Figures 4 and 5).

Figure 4

Figure 5

5. Finish the partial seam on the first rectangle (as indicated by the red line). Press the seam away from the embroidered block (Figure 6).

The block should measure 6˝ × 6˝ including seam allowances.

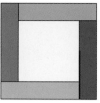

Figure 6

6. Repeat Steps 1–5 to frame all the embroidered blocks.

Construction

1. Lay out the blocks in alphabetical order with the message blocks in the corners.

2. Sew the blocks into rows.

3. Sew the rows together.

Borders

1. Referring to the quilt construction diagram (page 85), arrange and sew together 6 rectangles and 6 squares for each pieced side border. Add them to the quilt top.

2. Referring to the diagram, arrange and sew together 5 rectangles and 7 squares for each pieced top and bottom border. Add them to the quilt top.

3. Trim the inner borders and add them to the quilt top as shown in Borders (page 40).

4. Trim the outer borders and add them to the quilt top as shown in Borders.

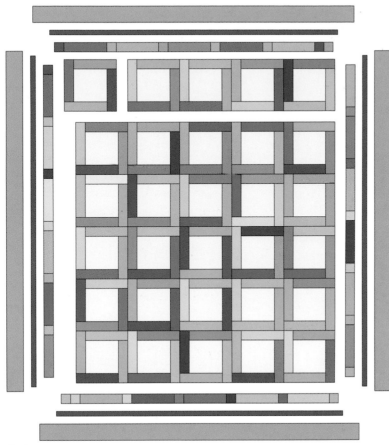

Quilt construction

Finishing

Layer, baste, quilt as desired, and bind (pages 41–43).

... And Puppy Dog Tails

A

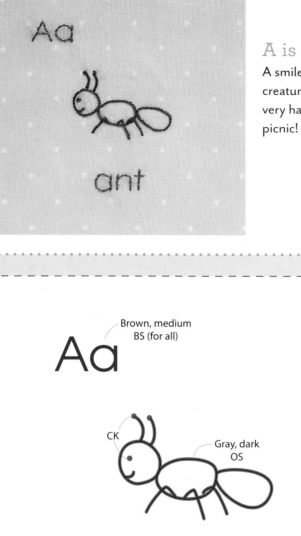

A is for Ant

A smile and alert antennae give this little creature instant personality. I imagine he is very happy because he's just spotted a lovely picnic!

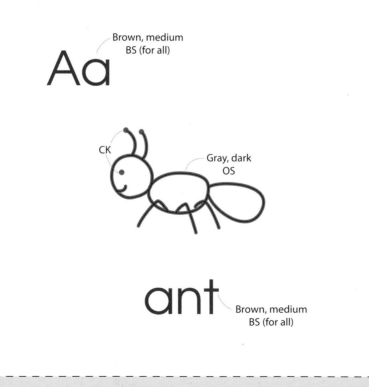

Brown, medium
BS (for all)

Aa

CK

Gray, dark
OS

ant
Brown, medium
BS (for all)

B is for Baseball

The fly stitch is perfect for creating the seam stitches of this baseball. For technical accuracy, I stitched the seams in opposite directions.

B

Bb

Brown, light
OS

Red
FS

baseball

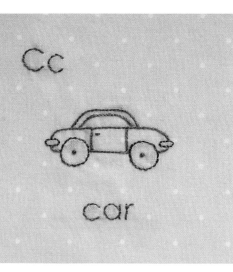

C is for Car

In the interest of simplicity, not all details are necessary. The door handle's position is the only indication of which direction the car is facing.

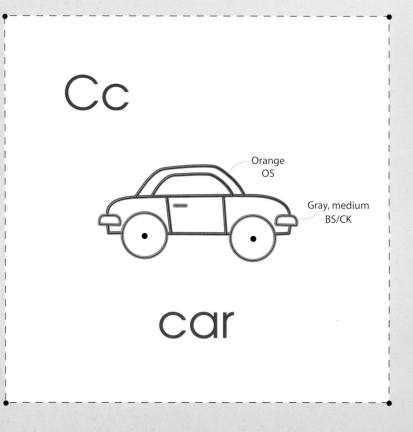

Orange
OS

Gray, medium
BS/CK

D is for Dinosaur

This prehistoric monster has no fearful characteristics because his face isn't visible. And yet his shape is very recognizable.

D

Gray, medium
OS

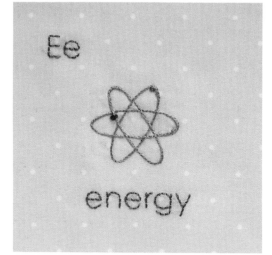

E is for Energy

Bring a touch of science using a classic icon.
Use 3 plies of floss for the colonial knots.

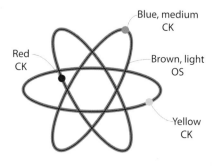

Ee

Blue, medium
CK

Red
CK

Brown, light
OS

Yellow
CK

energy

F is for Fort

This structure is made more interesting because it is set on an angle instead of facing the front, so you can see two sides of the fort. Little details like windows, a ladder, and flags give this design a lot of interest without being too complicated.

F

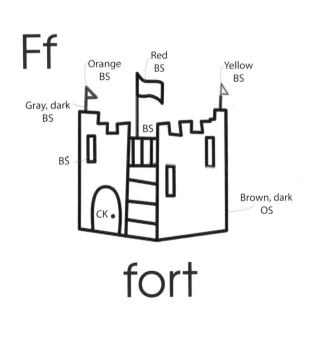

Ff

Orange BS

Red BS

Yellow BS

Gray, dark BS

BS

BS

Brown, dark OS

CK

fort

G

G is for Goal

Straight stitches made with only a single ply are very effective in creating realistic netting for this piece of sporting equipment. Stitch the ball first to make sure the stitches of the net are in the background. Use a stem stitch to contrast a little with the fine netting.

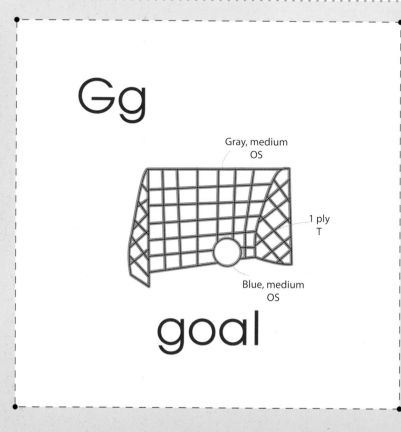

Gg

Gray, medium
OS

1 ply
T

Blue, medium
OS

goal

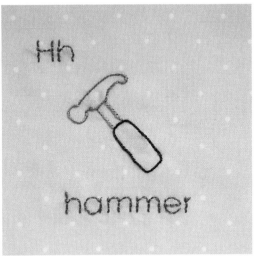

H is for Hammer

I used gray for the metal part of the hammer and a color for the handle to make this basic tool more interesting. By placing it on an angle, the hammer appears to be in motion.

H

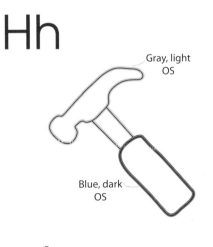

Hh

Gray, light
OS

Blue, dark
OS

hammer

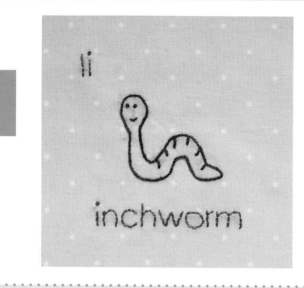

I is for Inchworm

The tiny inchworm is most easily recognized from its distinctive posture. The partial lines across its back give a hint of texture.

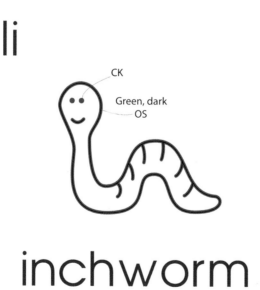

J is for Jacks

I think the game of jacks has become old-fashioned. But I marvel at how easy it is to re-create these tiny toys with only a few backstitches and colonial knots. They are graphically interesting and yet simple in detail.

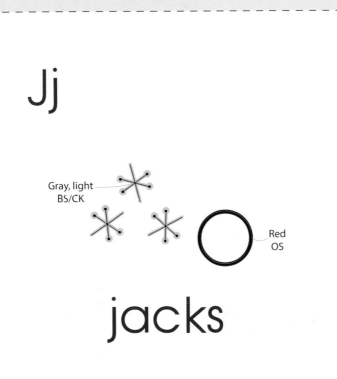

Jj

Gray, light
BS/CK

Red
OS

jacks

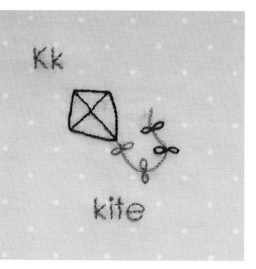

K is for Kite

Although wind is invisible, you can see it dancing playfully with this kite's decorated tail.

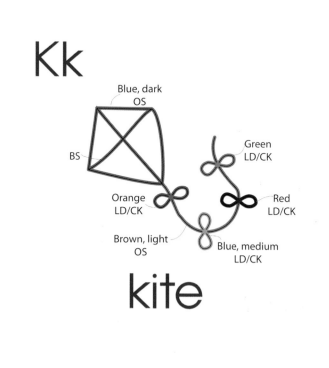

Kk

Blue, dark
OS

BS

Green
LD/CK

Orange
LD/CK

Red
LD/CK

Brown, light
OS

Blue, medium
LD/CK

kite

L is for Ladder

Most little boys I know love to climb. I thought including a ladder in this quilt would be fun. I also like how this ladder has a rough-hewn quality because the rungs are not perfectly straight. It looks handmade.

L

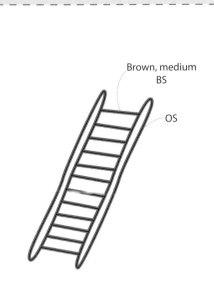

Ll

Brown, medium
BS

OS

ladder

M

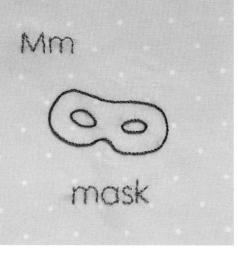

M is for Mask

Whether you're pretending to be the hero or the villain, a mask offers the perfect disguise.

Mm

Gray, dark
OS

mask

N is for Night

Night is the time to dream about yesterday's adventures and tomorrow's surprises.

Nn

Yellow OS

Orange TS

CK

night

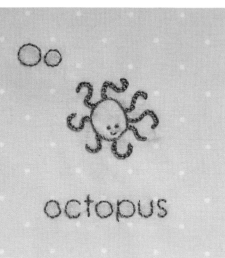

O is for Octopus

Once again, I have called the chain stitch into service because of its versatility. On this deep-sea creature, it suggests the suction cups on the tentacles.

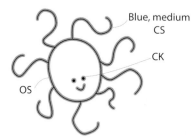

Oo

Blue, medium
CS

CK

OS

octopus

P is for Puppy

This happy animal looks like he's wagging his tail. The collar with a tag immediately turns him into a loved family pet. Stitch the face details with a single ply of dark gray.

P

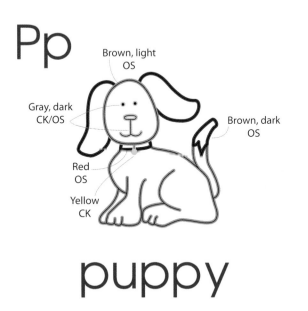

Pp

Brown, light
OS

Gray, dark
CK/OS

Brown, dark
OS

Red
OS

Yellow
CK

puppy

Q is for Quarter

It is interesting how the stem stitch and running stitch, along with the gray color, can add the perfect amount of texture and depth to this tiny replication of a metal object.

Qq

Gray, light
OS
RS
BS

25 ¢

quarter

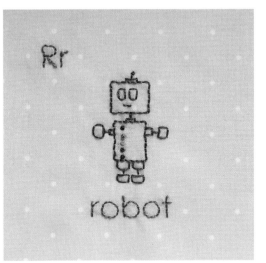

R is for Robot

Although this design has all the elements of a human, it clearly looks robotic because every feature is made with a straight line. I added the colorful knots to give the robot some animation—I think they look like blinking lights. And I stitched his mouth with a slight curve to suggest a smile, which makes him look friendly.

R

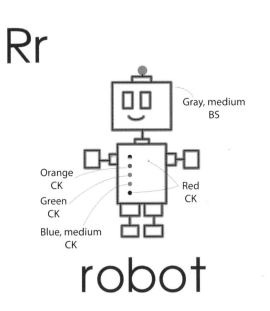

Gray, medium
BS

Orange
CK

Red
CK

Green
CK

Blue, medium
CK

S is for Snail

By twisting different brown floss threads together, the shell is much more interesting. It is very easy to get a sense of the natural color and texture variations in this tiny creature's home.

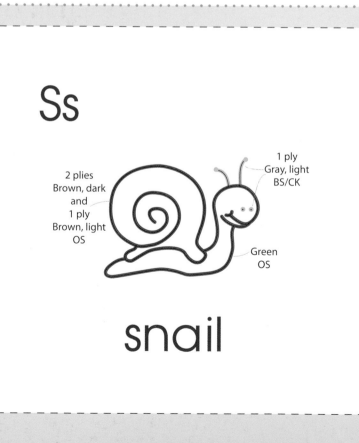

Ss

1 ply
Gray, light
BS/CK

2 plies
Brown, dark
and
1 ply
Brown, light
OS

Green
OS

snail

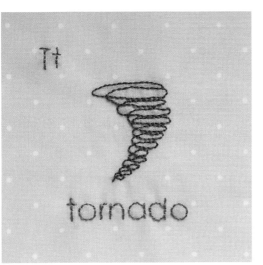

T is for Tornado

Some little boys really move through their days like a force of nature! I used a backstitch instead of my favored stem stitch for this twister to make the fine swirl details sharp and clear.

T

Tt

Gray, dark
BS

tornado

U

U is for Up

For this quilt, I have both minimal and ornate designs. This contrast and balance helps the eye move comfortably around the quilt. Obviously, this austere arrow is an example of a quiet design that is perfectly situated between two more elaborate images.

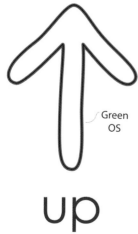

Green
OS

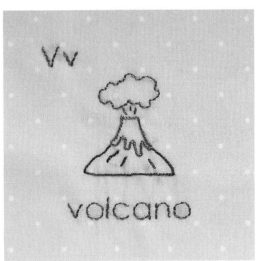

V is for Volcano

This active volcano is hard at work spewing lava and ash!

V

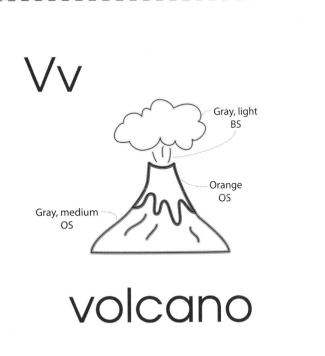

Vv

Gray, light
BS

Orange
OS

Gray, medium
OS

volcano

W is for Web

A web is very delicate, and this one is stitched entirely with a single ply of floss. I recommend stitching the couched swags in a spiral first, starting in the middle and working your way around to the outside end where the spider is hanging. Then add the backstitched spokes.

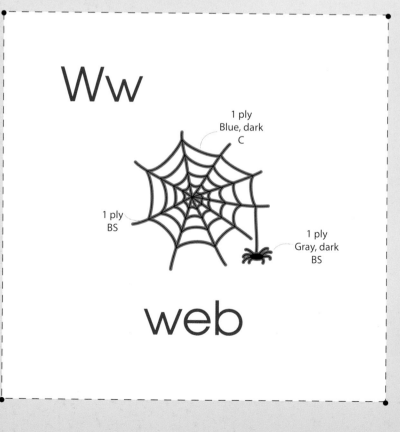

Ww

1 ply
Blue, dark
C

1 ply
BS

1 ply
Gray, dark
BS

web

X is for X Marks the Spot

Treasure maps really spark imaginations. This map looks tattered and mysterious with the torn and curled edges. I think this would be a fun image to enlarge and add many intriguing details, such as mountains and rivers and secret hiding places.

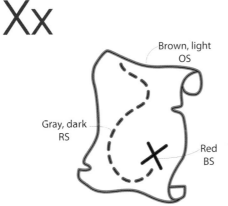

Brown, light
OS

Gray, dark
RS

Red
BS

Y is for Yo-Yo

I can imagine the secondary design that is created by the knots and straight stitches when this classic toy is spinning round and round and up and down.

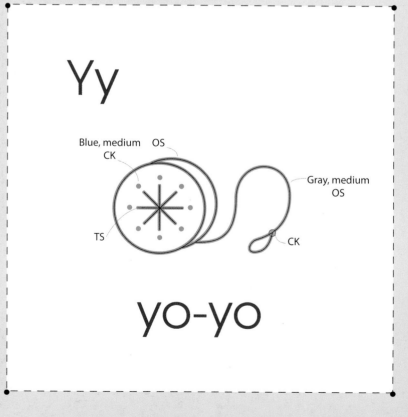

Z is for Zzz ...

I stitched the veins in the wing with a back-stitch to make them finer than the outline and to help lend a delicate quality to the wing. I also thought blue eyes would give this happy insect a little more personality.

Z

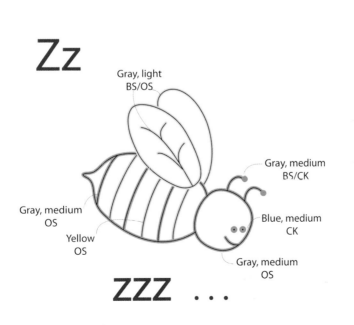

Zz

Gray, light
BS/OS

Gray, medium
BS/CK

Gray, medium
OS

Blue, medium
CK

Yellow
OS

Gray, medium
OS

ZZZ ...

Now I know my ABCs

Now I

Red
BS

know my

ABCs.

Next time won't you sing with me?

Next time
won't you

Green
BS

sing with

me?

Stitched with love

Orange
BS

For my darling boy

Boy

For my darling boy

Blue, medium
BS

Rainbow Dancers Framed Embroidery

YOU WILL NEED

COLOR	QUANTITY	COSMO #	DMC #
Pink, dark	1 skein	206	600
Pink, medium	1 skein	204	602
Pink, light	1 skein	353	605
Orange, dark	1 skein	146	740
Orange, medium	1 skein	145	742
Orange, light	1 skein	143	743
Yellow, dark	1 skein	302	444
Yellow, medium	1 skein	300	307
Yellow, light	1 skein	298	445
Green, dark	1 skein	273	702
Green, medium	1 skein	271	704
Green, light	1 skein	269	3819
Blue, dark	1 skein	414A	995
Blue, medium	1 skein	2412	3843
Blue, light	1 skein	412	996
Violet, dark	1 skein	2664	333
Violet, medium	1 skein	663	340
Violet, light	1 skein	662	3747
Purple, dark	1 skein	286	3837
Purple, medium	1 skein	284	208
Purple, light	1 skein	282	209

* 15˝ × 17˝ of background fabric for embroidery

* A store-bought frame to fit an 8½˝ × 11˝ photograph

Putting It Together

1. Complete the embroidery using the design (page 118). In each color, use dark for the bodice (SS), medium for the top ruffles (LD), light for the bottom ruffles (LD), and medium for the knots (CK). Use the 3 shades of each for the flowers (LD and CK) that radiate out from the tutus.

2. Press well.

3. Trim the embroidery to fit the frame.

4. Fit the embroidery into the frame as if it were a photograph.

Soft Blocks

Finished size: 3½˝ × 3½˝ × 3½˝

YOU WILL NEED

For one block:

* 1 square 6˝ × 6˝ for embroidery

* 5 squares 4˝ × 4˝ of assorted fabrics

* Polyester stuffing

For letter patterns, see pages 138–142.

The alphabet offers all sorts of design ideas. Stitch up the entire alphabet, just the first few letters, or the letters of a child's name.

Putting It Together

1. Complete the embroidery on the 6˝ × 6˝ square using the letter patterns (pages 138–142). Trim it to 4˝ × 4˝ (see Trimming Embroidered Blocks, pages 30–33).

2. On the wrong side of all 6 fabric squares, use a pencil to mark ¼˝ away from each corner (Figure 1).

3. Sew 2 squares together, starting and stopping at the ¼˝ mark. Always backstitch a few stitches to reinforce the seam at both ends (Figure 2).

4. Add the remaining 4 squares as shown. Start and stop every seam at a ¼˝ mark and always sew a few reinforcing stitches at both ends of every seam (Figure 3).

5. To form the block, match and sew seams 1, 2, 3, and 4 (Figure 4).

6. Sew 2 of the remaining sides and leave the third side open.

7. Turn the block right side out, fill it with stuffing, and hand stitch the opening closed.

Figure 1

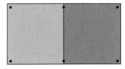

Figure 2

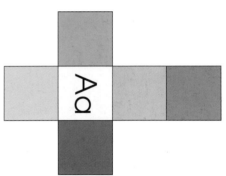

Figure 3

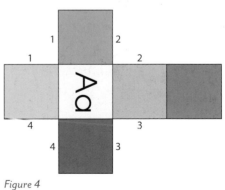

Figure 4

Traffic Framed Embroidery

YOU WILL NEED

COLOR		QUANTITY	COSMO #	DMC #
■	Red	1 skein	108	150
■	Green	1 skein	633	439
■	Blue	1 skein	733	932
■	Brown, light	1 skein	892	3023
■	Gray, dark	1 skein	368	3790

* A 15˝ × 17˝ rectangle of background fabric for embroidery

* A store bought-frame to fit an 8½˝ × 11˝ photograph

Putting It Together

1. Complete the embroidery using the design at right.

2. Press well.

3. Trim the embroidery to fit the frame.

4. Fit the embroidery into the frame as if it were a photograph.

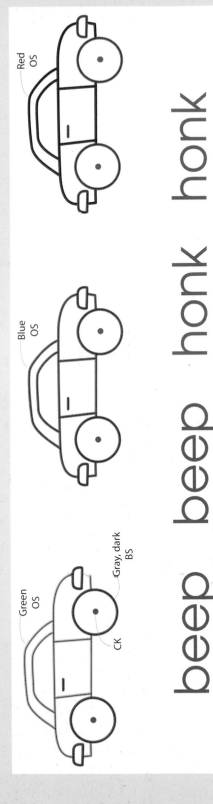

9-Patch Robot Pillow

Finished size: 12˝ × 12˝

YOU WILL NEED

* 9 squares 4½˝ × 4½˝ of assorted fabrics

* 2 strips ¾˝ × 4˝ and 2 strips ¾˝ × 4½˝ for embroidered block border

* 1 square 13˝ × 13˝ for backing

* 2 pieces of batting 13˝ × 13˝

* Polyester stuffing

Putting It Together

1. Complete the embroidery on one square using the R is for Robot pattern (page 103). Trim it to 4˝ × 4˝ (see Trimming Embroidered Blocks, pages 30–33).

2. Sew the 4˝ inner border strips to the sides of the embroidered square (Figure 1). Then sew the 4½˝ inner border strips to the top and bottom of the square (Figure 2).

Figure 1

Figure 2

3. Lay out the 8 remaining fabric squares and the embroidered square.

4. Sew the squares into rows (Figure 3).

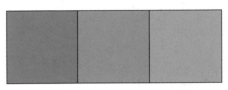
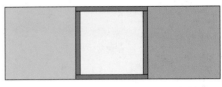

Figure 3

5. Sew the rows together.

6. Layer, baste, and quilt (page 41) the front of the pillow to a piece of batting, and then do the same with the back, using the other piece of batting.

7. Lay the pillow front and back right sides together and pin around the edges.

8. Sew a ¼˝ seam all the way around the pillow, leaving a 5˝ opening along the bottom edge. Trim the corner seam allowances.

9. Turn the pillow right side out and press the edges. Then fill the pillow with stuffing to the desired fullness.

10. Hand stitch the opening closed.

Zinnia Pillow

Finished size: 12˝ × 12˝

YOU WILL NEED

* 1 square 10˝ × 10˝ for embroidered block

* 4 strips 2½˝ × 12½˝ of assorted fabrics for frame

* 1 square 13˝ × 13˝ for backing

* 2 pieces of batting 13˝ × 13˝

* Polyester stuffing

Putting It Together

1. Complete the embroidery on one square using the Z is for Zinnia pattern (page 75) enlarged 500%. Trim it to 8˝ × 8˝ (see Trimming Embroidered Blocks, pages 30-33).

2. To add the frame, follow Steps 2–5 of ... *And Puppy Dog Tails*, Pieced Blocks (pages 82 and 84). The block should measure 12½˝ × 12½˝ with seam allowances.

3. Layer, baste, and quilt (page 41) the front of the pillow to a piece of batting, and then do the same with the back, using the other piece of batting.

4. Lay the pillow front and back right sides together and pin around the edges. Sew a ¼˝ seam all the way around the pillow, leaving a 5˝ opening along the bottom edge. Trim the corner seam allowances.

5. Turn the pillow right side out and press the edges. Then fill the pillow with stuffing to the desired fullness.

6. Hand stitch the opening closed.

FRAMED EMBROIDERY
GALLERY

Here are a few more ideas for quick, affordable, and beautiful art. Picture frames of many shapes, sizes, colors, and styles are very easy to find.

These ideas were designed to fit standard frame sizes, but every design in this book can be enlarged or reduced to be any size you like.

Choose a fabric you like and cut a piece that is at least 2˝ larger on all sides for easy stitching.

A shadow box makes just about anything look important. I enlarged the angel wing design 150% and embroidered it onto a soft, neutral linen. The letters for the name are not enlarged and are stitched on a separate piece of linen. Then I frayed the edges for an added detail.

Enlarge a design to fit the frame. The P is for Puppy design (page 101) was enlarged 200% to fit in a 5˝ × 7˝ frame. Personalize with the name of a beloved family pet.

I like the look of a small object, like this little black purse, in a larger frame.

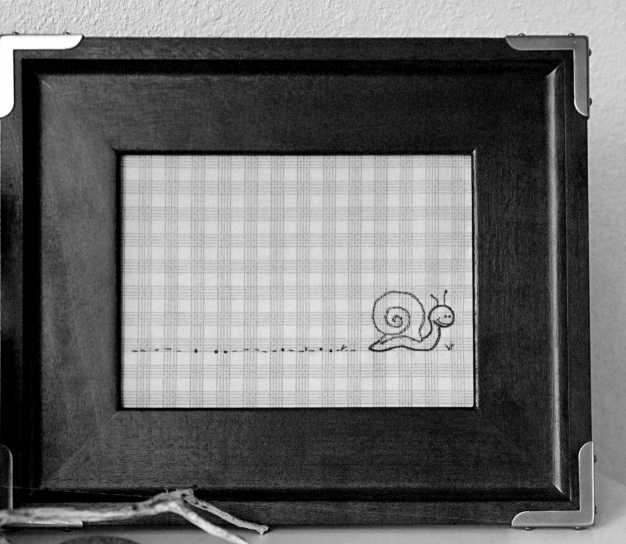

You don't always have to center an object in a frame. This little snail has slowly crawled from one edge of the frame to the other and is about to disappear! Embellish the design as you like. I added a few simple knots and straight stitches behind the snail to suggest the trail he made behind him.

EMBROIDERING
PREMADE ITEMS

*Consider changing the word under the design to
suit the application, or omit the word altogether.*

Lighter clothes, like this pair of boy's shorts, are easier to trace on than darker clothes.

Add your own caption—you might have a special family good-night saying that would be nice to stitch.

Nighty Night

Sweet Dreams

Repeating the same design in different colors turns these ordinary store-bought table linens into very festive, and functional, party decorations.

Remember to use a stabilizer backing when stitching on stretchy fabric, such as this jersey knit dress.

Alphabets

Aa Bb
Cc Dd
Ee Ff

Gg Hh
Ii Jj Kk Ll
Mm Nn
Oo Pp

Qq Rr

Ss Tt Uu

Vv Ww

Xx Yy Zz

S is for Stitch ·

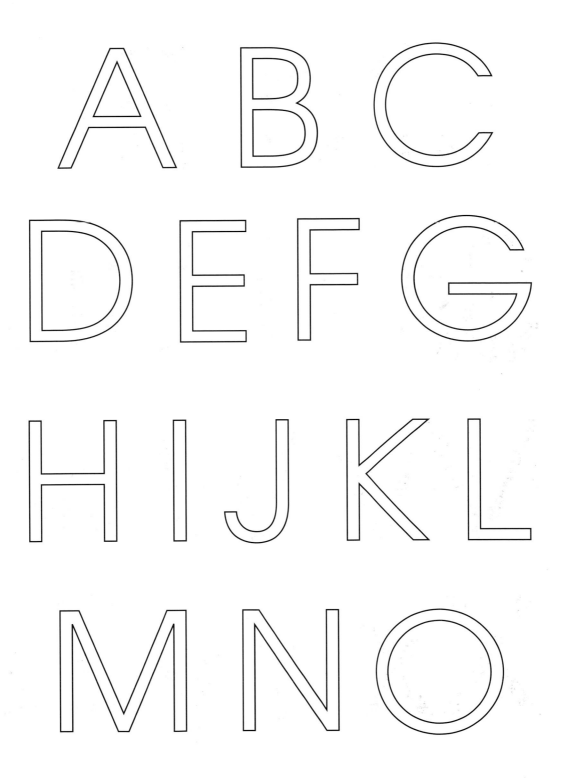

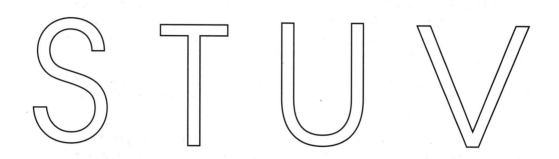

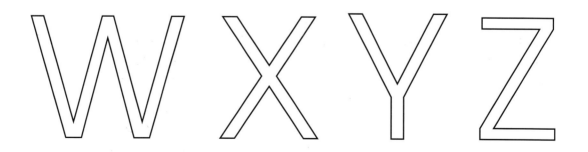

About the Author

Photo by Maggie Linder

Kristyne Czepuryk's thinks her life is a cliché.

She married her high school sweetheart, enjoyed a short career before becoming a stay-at-home mom and her favorite color is pink.

Adding to her rather ordinary biography, she survived the usual hardships of being a middle child and took piano lessons; she was a Girl Guide (she's Canadian, by the way), participated in assorted recreational sports (at which she did badly) and learned to work with a needle and thread from her mother and aunt. She preferred creative activities—sewing, crafting, scrapbooking ... and still does.

After earning an English degree, she went back to school, got a public relations diploma and became employable. However, her first real job required her to do things like on-camera interviews—as in "Live at 5, film at 11." She figured out pretty fast that she was so not cut out for that. She found something behind the scenes, writing manuals—the computer, policy, procedure, and training type. ... (yawn). Before she had time to find something else that satisfied her creativity, however, she became a mom. Twice.

Then something happened. She made herself a pretty diaper bag—without a pattern. Then she made another. And another. She didn't realize it at the time, but she was becoming a pattern designer.

Today she calls herself a wife, mom, pattern designer/writer, teacher, blogger and owner of a little sewing pattern business called "Pretty by Hand". You can find her patterns and blog at prettybyhand.com.

Supplies/Resources

Fabric and Embroidery Floss
Lecien USA

lecienusa.com

Needles
Jeana Kimball's Foxglove Cottage
jeanakimballquilter.com/store/

Longarm Quilting
Angela Walters
quiltingismytherapy.com

Tools

* Gingher Scissors and Shears
gingher.com

* Olfa
olfa.com

* Decorative pins
Annie Kight
etsy.com/shop/pinksandneedles

Garments

* Old Navy
oldnavy.com

* Walmart
walmart.com

Frames and Linens

* HomeSense
homesense.com

* IKEA
ikea.com

* Michaels Stores, Inc.
michaels.com